Bethany W. Pope is a UK-ba
Southern United States. She
Scotland, the Philippines
Virginia, Kansas, Texas an
current home in Wiltshire.

She lived in an orphanage for three years before dropping
out of high-school, but later continued her education at
Mary Baldwin College where she earned her BA in English
Literature. She went on to earn her Master's Degree in
Creative Writing from University of Wales Trinity Saint
David and her PhD in Creative Writing from Aberystwyth
University.

She writes constantly, is madly in love with her husband
Matthew David Clarke, and spends at least three hours a
week Skyping with her family.

She has been published in *Ampersand, Anon, Art Times, The
AWP, Blue Tattoo, The Hidden, The Writers' Hub* and in *De/
Tached*, an anthology published by Parthian. She was the
winner of the inaugural Luigi Bonomi Associates Prize for
Fiction in 2007 and was shortlisted for a Faulkner–Wisdom
Award in 2010.

Her blog is at sinetimorepress.wordpress.com

Bethany Pope's compelling debut collection *A Radiance* weaves the voices of four generations into a rich story of family betrayal and survival, shame and grace, the visceral and the sublime. Unafraid to mine the darkest, most intimate and most radiant aspects of human experience, Pope's poetry gives glimpses into a world both contemporary and deeply attuned to history – the embattled history of a family, but also of the American South where the author grew up. A sense of offbeat wonder at everyday miracles of survival and love both fires these poems and haunts them – in the best possible way.

Tiffany S. Atkinson
Author of *Kink and Particle* and *Catulla et al*

The central image of Bethany Pope's collection is a tin of army surplus uranium buried by her grandfather in the back yard. A similar weird light, dangerous and beautiful, illuminates these poems of family history, love and childhood. An exhilarating and exceptional new voice in poetry.

Matthew Francis
Author of *Blizzard*, *Dragons*, *Whereabouts*,
Mandeville and *WHOM*

This is a stunning debut collection. It seems as if nothing has escaped her gaze: from uranium hidden light to the 'roots, which grow from watching'. Like the blade of her ancestor's knife, her pen, too, cuts a fine feast of welcome at the kitchen table. In a lacerated world of experience, these poems invite us to reinvent loss as a new kind of dwelling, where the infinitesimal becomes as luminous as ever. The stories shared also remind us that the past never fully disappears.

Menna Elfyn
Author of *Aderyn Bach Mewn Llaw,*
Eucalyptus and *Cell Angel*

A RADIANCE

Also by Bethany W. Pope

The Life of Dogs (Createspace 2011)
Forthcoming *Persephone in the Underworld*
(Rufus Books 2016)

A RADIANCE

BETHANY W. POPE

Cultured Llama Publishing

First published in 2012 by
Cultured Llama Publishing
11 London Road
Teynham, Sittingbourne
ME9 9QW
www.culturedllama.co.uk

A CIP record for this book is available from The British Library

ISBN 978-0-9568921-3-3

Printed in Great Britain by Lightning Source UK Ltd

Contents

For Ruth and Dan

What We Know

Daniel Ball, the farmer's son,
fell for the girl on the veranda;
a catlike child with auburn hair
and a wistful, deep-blue expression.

He had been a sharp-shooter in Japan
        before trading guns for desk,
filing away the bodies and coming home to a lifetime free
from K-rations. His mother made him fried squirrel for
        breakfast,
the meat sending up its sweetish smell, garnished with apple
and sliced green onion and pink squares of quivering Spam.

The light dancing in her thick dark bun, on the clean iron range,
on the tattered yellow wallpaper which clung to the walls,
impeccably clean, scrubbed, but smelling of hickory smoke
and the fat of old meals. He ate his food with polite grunts,
washed at the pump and dressed clean and creased as always.

He left his tiny mother in the doorway,
dressed in blue homespun
and rubber galoshes, gathering
breadcrumbs to feed to the hens.

He knew a few places in town that were hiring; the sheriff
needed deputies, the lawyer wanted clerks, and Ole' Doc,
the mine owner and sole town physician, had posted notices
for supervisors down in the pits.

He could perform well at all three tasks, but the sunlight
called to him, the scent of trees and summer heat
were things he could not live without, and so
he set his face to the surface jobs before
        nosing down the well.

The surface was not made for people such as him.
Ole'Doc saw the soldier for an interview in the office
of his home. Dan stood, hat-in-hand, on the far side of an oaken
desk of hundred-year lineage decorated with fragmented
biology

bobbing up and down in alcoholic jars. His eyes were
caught by
a two-headed fetus, four arms and four legs sharing a spine,
and his own back crawled at so much inescapable unity,
as deadly as unwanted love.

He thought it the impersonal punishment of biology,
not yet having met even a fragment of God, and still
he felt in sympathy
the tickling of a ghost twin interlocking its vertebrae
in the spaces of his spine.
Ole'Doc smiled at him from the safety of successful sixty
years, a man

grown rich and fat from other hands than his. On his
desk stood
a collection of picture frames, carved heavy silver,
bearing a succession
of images spanning nearly forty years. His children. Mary,
the eldest, wed eighteen years ago to a boy her father chose.

Her face was beautiful and hard, her husband's hand
laid on an arm that even through the photograph,
itched to draw away from him. Four boys, all doctors,
working hard in other towns and waiting for inheritance.

And finally the youngest, a girl carelessly dressed and
        obviously superfluous,
in her late teenage years. Looking at that image, Dan felt
        an undeniable
frisson, and had difficulty swallowing his flowing
        saliva when Ole' Doc,
his new-signed boss, held out his hand.

In a moment of prolepsis the old man grunted,
'Welcome aboard, son. May we have many long
days together, and cool, clear nights.' Dan nodded
his thanks, replaced his hat, and took his leave.

Trouble met him on the porch, beneath the flowering
        scuppernong,
those large blue eyes, older than her years, that lithe, soft body.
It was that same old story, archetypal pattern:
two young lovers meet in inauspicious circumstance,

joined twin-like at the heart. Made separate by race,
by class, by the presence or lack of new green money.
In stories such as this, what do details matter?
They met, they loved,
they drew each other from the paths they would have chosen.
They lived.

White Wedding

You were married in December, at nineteen-
years-old, against your families wishes.
You dropped out of school,
and abandoned
what the Ole'Doc planned for your future.
You were always his favourite, his good Ruth,
and yet, when they opened their home
for reception and for ceremony
you thought they offered mercy with the swan-
shaped napkins and third-class Champagne.
You knew nothing then, about high flavours,
and had no way of knowing they thought
even that swill was too good for you.

The dress, visible to the guests, the outside world,
was custom made to fit your body,
the last of that kind, and far from the first.
Your mother hired a dressmaker special,
emphasised the silk and organdy, implying
your loss of status in a way that was only
a reflection on you, through language of colour;
more yellow than white.

Your friends from school were not invited,
nor anyone that you particularly liked.
The groom, Dan, and his family were the sole
exceptions. They stood in that red-silked room
in a benevolent cluster of health in that cancerous cell.

Dan's mother, a few years
older than your eldest sister,
stood small and dark in the corner,
near your father's warped heart,

which floated malignant in the jar on the bookshelf,
bluish and air-starved, from want of fresh blood.

You broke, like your namesake,
        from the grip of your parents,
your mother's strong hand left red marks on your bicep
as you tore free to join the authors of your man.
They had prepared a bed for you in their home.
Then you would lay in it, though you would not sleep.

There was music, the made-harsh voice
of your father's strained violin, playing
the glasslike songs he favoured, the crystal
Age of Reason music with no room for a soul
in its cutting edge. But you hardly heard it,
missing the message, the vicious incision
that excised you from their life.

You told me, sixty years later, something
that had never really left your mind. After
the brief party, when you had returned
the borrowed dress to your mother – she hoarded it
for years in the draughty attic, until the fabric
rotted out – your new father-in-law sidled up
to fetch you home. He was an old farmer, like Dan,
tall, quiet, dark, and his rough hand touched
your arm more gently than your own blood ever had.

He steered you out into the snow-filled
driveway, towards his rusty truck, dying
of the salt your father spread to grip his new tyres.
Before he opened up your door, before
ushering you across that threshold,
he hugged you close, and told you this:

'If my boy, or anybody, ever hits you,
or touches you in any way you don't like,
you come out, or call loud to get me,
and I'll come running to shoot them, right
down dead. You are my daughter,
the child of my heart. And Dan is gonna
treat you right, like you deserve.
You see if he don't.'

You never did forget that moment,
you treasure it enough at least
to tell me with a light in your eyes,
as though afraid of losing memory
forever, your girlish, laughing music,
telling me, though you do not know it,
of the first time in your life
you were ever really loved.

Christmas at Grandmother's

Three-year-old John sits perched on hard horsehair,
a low embroidered stool whose leonine feet,
that frightening Chippendale Ball-and-claw,
face their talons toward the dense-papered corner of the wall.

The Christmas tree glows with enormous
white bulbs, which even at this distance
bake their waves against his neck, a crisping radiation,
though John is not allowed to see the laden boughs.
He has been clinging to Grandmother again,
and deserves what he gets.

Food, a bed with clean sheets, clothes that are better
than Danny and the baby get at home with
Ruth, better than the rags worn by the rest of the town,
who are not of the family. They took in the boy,
a spare heir to nothing with a name that is not theirs,
or belonging to any of the important players,
a name unattached to moneyed family,
unable, like poor Ruthie, to stand on his own
without the benefit of family money.

If John misses his mommy, he shall see her
soon enough. The Popes are coming tomorrow,
for dinner. The spying town will see them enter,
dressed in their best and still looking shameful.
Ruth with the haircut she gave to herself,
the failed rolled permanent, the baby hanging
from her teat like a hillbilly's suckling, draining her out
sow-like, because formula costs more at the company store
and there is no family discount, not even for
the owner's prodigal daughter.

Small Danny looked peaked yesterday
when grandmother came on them in town,
a little anaemic, in need of some medicine
stronger than a smile, a hard pinch on the cheek. She smiles
to recall it. And that man she thwarted Father for;
failed sheriff, failed farmer, Billy Ball, that shiftless
half-Indian, will speak to Doc in bitter cultivated tones,
of foot-on-throat subservience, his hands visibly trembling
suppressing the urge to wolf up the meat that his starved-
coyote nature hungers for.

Grandmother has sent down orders to the kitchen:
cook the beef rare, with plenty of juice,
serve with greasy-beans and potato au gratin,
for dessert a good, cream-laden pie.
John has fed up nicely, as he should, isn't that why
his loving parents farmed him out? To save him
looking weak? To show the town their forgiveness, the level
of their mercy? To show it all, and well, to Ruth?

It is a pity that they haven't more room,
or they would have taken John and Danny both.
But one is work enough, and the boy is so demanding,
always whining to be held. Grandmother knows
how tiresome it gets. And although her daughter
has resisted her training, the man she ran off with
has learned fast and well. He hardly looked at John-
Nelson the last time they met in town, and Danny,
thin, ratty, she savours reliving it, spat on his young
brother's clothes and pushed him down in the road.

Grandmother had to stoop to brush him off.
It was a fall he paid for later when
she caught him under the fir tree
in the living room, smearing grubby fingers
on the hard red feathers of her Florentine blown-
glass birds. This is her payment for kindness.

Christmas is tomorrow, and the boy is still,
shifting on horsehair as quietly as he can.
His knee hurts from falling, and he aches
someplace else, but there isn't any use
in crying. And his world is not desolate.

There are other birdies to look at, printed,
they rise from the paper, all golden and red.
They are not like any other birds that John
has ever seen in town proper, or even in books.
Their feathers curl in lyre shapes
which he has no word for, and their painted
beaks are open in throat-trilling song
that can never cease or be stepped on.

He sings with them, quietly,
avoiding detection. Her hearing is good,
but she cannot hear this. Tomorrow night
is Christmas. His family will be here.
There will be time to rejoice.

Waiting Rooms

They sit in second-class to Nashville, Danny pressing
his narrow face against the cool, smeared glass
watching the trees, the strip-mines, the telephone poles.
Tar-sided shacks, like his own house, thrust their outhouses
train-side revealing the occasional naked bum.

Ruth intermittently insists on the mastication of cream
cheese smeared on a graham cracker, to maintain
his small strength. She eats nothing herself,
but spends a quarter to rent her son a blood-
stained cotton pillow from the uniformed conductor
who bruises her knee with the corner of his wheeled
tray and calls her 'Ma'am' grudgingly,
        beneath sly, lowered eyes.

She bends down while Danny sleeps, to feel
his breathing and reassure herself of the continued
beating of his heart. While he sleeps she reads mysteries,
chronicling murders and the exploits of the insane,
or tries to, when she can persuade herself
to cease her faithless checking.

They pull in mid-morning; Dan is slow to wake,
it takes his heart awhile to get the starved blood flowing.
She bundles him first onto the platform, then
into a taxi, closest to the curb, driven by a black man,
the first non-white that she has ever seen who was not a hired
chauffer. By the time they arrive he is well woken up.

A dove-hatted nurse collects them at reception,
winging the sick boy into a wheelchair with muted
reproach, 'Didn't your doctor tell you he shouldn't be walking?'

'No, Daddy said to get him here, my brother Roddy
agreed. They didn't say how, and you'd think
they would have if it had been important,
they've both been in practice so long.' With such
sputtered fragments Ruth clings to her dignity.

The nurse, white garbed, replies with her spine,
pointing her sharp bones at Ruth, wheeling Danny
through padded metal doors. The noise summons
company. Another older nurse pecks in, long nosed,
bifocaled, across linoleum counter-top saying, 'You'd better
go home now, dear. Visiting hours have ended for today.
Return tomorrow, between ten and one
and we'll pencil you in to have words with the doctor.'

This nurse, though kinder, has no way of knowing that home
is seventy miles away. And Ruth has just enough
money to stay a week in a moderate hotel,
without eating, or two weeks in a cheaper one,
feeding herself on canned beans and reconstituted
franks, which she calls weenies, more plastic than meat.

They can just pay for this surgery,
though this stretching relieves her, in a way. She did not
have to slink to her mother on her belly, the way
the high-toned lady wants her to.
She does not have to beg.

Twelve years of poverty have not prepared her
for this. Yes, she is dressed cheaply, the navy fabric of her best
suit shiny and tacky-looking along the seat,
bought at discount off the rack and self-altered. It
is still a shock for a girl who came up without dressing
herself, each garment the best quality, handmade
by experts to fit her lithe shape. It is still a shock
to be so undervalued.

To have one suit for church, this best one, and a house
dress only. Each hung on a peg and hand washed after wearing.
It is a shock to see her white hands grown so red,
or the sour smell Dan gets in the morning after
a night spent hard-drinking with the boys from the mine
who are making more, but can afford it even less.
She still thinks each morning
that she might wake up to sunlight seeing a uniformed
Irish girl, smiling, wielding a tray, ready to wait on her.

And it is difficult to forget
that at eighteen years old, even here, away from home,
both nurses would have deferred to her, recognising class
by her clothing, by the way her body had been held,
that cold tone she inherited from her mother and can still
occasionally bring out. These farm girls would have
trembled, scraping, making every answer 'Yes'.
She tries not to calculate the cost of her marriage,
she tries, every day, to maintain her worth without
thinking, or if she must, thinking only of her injured son
who makes it worth it. Her eldest, heartbroken Danny.

The room she finds her body in makes this resolution
more difficult to hold. It smells of mould and rotten plaster,
and the fat girl at the counter hasn't any teeth.
She drapes breasts the consistency of whey
        cheese across the countertop and breathlessly, insists
that if a *friend* were to join Ruth in her bedroom
later, she would not look, or draw back the office shades.

Surgery in two days, and then, hopefully, recovery.
Two weeks more and her small store of love
will pack up again, facing south, and this time driving
in a Ford held together with metal wire balling,
spit, a slather of grease. Less than a month,

no matter what happens here, and the survivors
will be driving. It took nine-hundred miles worth of looking
For Dan to reach space untouched by his father-
in-law's fingers and find viable work.

Ruth focuses on this. Faint hope.
It is better than seeing the fluid-stained mattress
she sits upon, or thinking of food she cannot,
and yet must, bring herself to eat. She does not
think about families, or flaws of the heart.
She reads Agatha Christie.

Ruth, willfully, does not think that sometimes
further injury, incision, removals, the bright smell,
of saline, a change of the blood, are necessary
for new growth. She has always been one
to let the pus build. She does not think.
She sits encased in other people's foulness,
reading her mysteries, in a small,
dark-chambered room, throbbing with stench.
Waiting for light.

Last Calls

Twelve-year-old Danny stands on the stairs,
his hole-socked feet hanging over the edge,
balancing between bathroom and hall.

His brother is sleeping in their double bed,
adenoidal snores filling the air, but that is not
what woke him, it was the sound of brakes
and unsure tyres squealing in the humid air.

Danny is used to this, he knows what is coming,
and in the wake of Mom's silence and wide, tired eyes,
this has become solely his duty, the eldest-child's job.

He knows that his mother is in her bedroom, waiting,
wrapped in cheap nylon bedspread, auburn
hair messy and frazzled, the cilia fear-raised on her
narrow arms. This is how she waits for love.

And this is how her Danny protects it.
Outside the door, the sound of wheels
squealing on grass, the metallic crump

of a fast-opened door. Buddy, the spaniel, barks once,
then whimpers, silenced by a kick to the ribs, Danny's
paternal namesake turns the knob on the door.
It is three a.m. and he has had too much to drink.

He staggers in, dark haired and waltzing
in a liquored broken rhythm, his clothes smell
like fermented sugar, dark and sour-sweet.

Danny, unafraid, knows what is coming
and his cotton-slick feet know every stair,
he slinks down, sweaty-palmed, gripping
the bannister while his Daddy slams the kitchen

door. Danny finds him at the sway-backed table,
his head ensconced in dark-skinned arms
fitting perfectly the low warp in the board.

He has vomited, a little, and it pools around his head
in a strong-smelling pocket. Danny fills a glass of cool
water at the sink, and feeds his father Anacin from
his own small hand, unsurprised when his Daddy

reaches up to grip him. He blows his stomach-
stenched breath in the boy's open face, saying,
'Danny. Danny. Never again.' The boy shuts

his mother's blue eyes, nodding, believing
not a single word. He says, 'Come on,
let's get you to Mom's room.' And offers
his shoulder as a brace for his father to rise.

The man staggers up, saying, 'No, Dan, I mean it.
I can't stand to see myself like this, and the hurt
in her eyes is more than rebuke. I'm killing her love.'

'It's just the jobs, boy. That awful lack.
It's awful hard to be a man when stuck under a shadow.
The weight always on me, my blood and her family.
I am proving them right.'

Danny understands each word, individually,
but strung together they make little sense.
All he knows is that it has been years since his father
kept steady hours, his cousins call him half-breed,

and while he is not sure what honour is,
he knows the feel of jagged edge around
the hole where it once was. He does not know

how much the next six months will teach him.
He does not know, and cannot comprehend,
that he will see his father sink down as far
as he is now every night for half a year, before

he realises that the tight, soured squeeze in his guts
is not his usual delicate illness, but the rancid glow of shame.
On the night he does he will not offer solace, or comfort

for his father's pain. He will leave his father there, table bound,
encased in vomit, shuddering through the coolest hours
of the night, waking unable to stomach his waffles. His father
will not reproach him for leaving him like this, but he will stare.

And after a stretch of vile sleep he wakes
raising up his head to face the busy morning,
gazing over John-Nelson's head
        and past his silent tight-mouthed wife
at his oldest boy whose sullen chewing seems to say, 'My God,
you are pathetic.' His stomach heaves with bile.

Radiance

I have seen photographs
describing a fragment
of the way they were then,
my uncle and father,
Danny and John.
The doctor of not-yet,
the future minister,
dressed country presentable,
more fifties than sixties,
with scrimped hair cut high and tight,
spiked by their grandfather
who couldn't stand a handbreadth of locks
on the head of a boy.
It was their first year in Florida

inhabiting a home I came to know well,
when I lived there, half grey-blue wood,
half brick and painted cinderblock;
that wide, sprawling yard of hibiscus,
myrtle, orange trees – still replete
with elephant ear that Popie had not vanquished –
ferns, the square rose garden in the corner
their father never gave up on,
to spite the environment, that light sandy soil
so different from mountains
where if the land was sweet, where
you'd drop a flower and a shrub would flourish,
fed by unseen source.

The boys were curious, a little too daring.
I have no idea where they found
the magazine which sold Army Surplus.
I've no idea where they came up with the cash,
but somehow or other they scrimped it together,

along with stamped envelope, an address card
messily filled in by dyslexic hands.

I could not have stood the waiting they endured,
all those weeks of processing. Their little card
filtering through the guts
of some vast company,
denuded of its sweat stained,
green florals. Knowing my father's
life-long impatience he probably hounded
the postman to ruinous depression ,
wondering out loud, when the poor man
showed his overheated adult face,
if the package had been missed.

Eventually it came round,
as all things do,
wrapped in brown paper,
addressed by hand.
Danny was older, his privilege to open,
sliding his knife blade scalpel-like through twine,
revealing a small round can,
the kind home-movie film came in,
sealed off tight.

John was the one to uncover the sacrament,
and what shone there alone in the bottom,
naturally inspired
religious awe and adoration.
It lit up his face like a mosaic veil
and made brother Danny
fall back as though stricken.
John sucked in his breath.

A small disc of incredible radiation,
a glowing light that could never be

extinguished or hidden,
that the boys, or anyone,
could never make dwindle
or in any way diminish.
Light without heat, that anyway
burned them,
a host of slow poison to hold on the palm.

They stood alone together,
made isolate by silence,
hands of the same size and substance
clasped, impressed with sharp nails
that could belong to either of them.

They never really played with it.
Popie came in from his job
reclaiming the neglected, placing the broken,
the brain-damaged, deranged
in jobs that they could handle,
according to capacity.
He saw the light, and knew what it was.

He did not yell, or strike them.
He did not even cover it with can-lid.
He knelt down,
hands that struggled at nurturing
settling down on twin curvatures of spine.
He laid out the danger
there on the table, home to toxic feast
and familial rite of pleasure at meals.

When he had finished
describing his horror
my father reached out,
white-cheeked, trembling,
his eyelids glistening,

raw and bright.
He closed the lid tight.

There was already treasure
in that yard.
They added worth
by burying this surfeit.
The boys dug down
deep to plant this seed,
shovels flying
until they hit the water table.

They set it down,
like Hebrew priests
willfully forgetting
the location of the Ark,
willfully forgetting that power
such as this
has a way of seeping out.

The light, Springish,
like the sun seen through leaves,
never went out.
It is glowing still, somewhere,
waiting to be found.
Eventually, when I lived there,
I would seek it out.

In the places I looked I found:
a roundel of imported flint,
a similar chunk of rose quartz,
the soggy remains of Popie's first garden,
the spilled ancient slag
of a conquistador foundry,
the skull of a large dog,
a horse tooth,

five ring-neck serpents, still alive,
and the rusted husk
of a Volkswagen side mirror.

I am still looking,
still scouring the depths
for that dangerous light,
which I have never seen,
though I have felt its intimations.
I have faith I shall do,
when the time is right.
In the meantime I will pray
for the recovery of light.[1]

---

1   In the early 1960s it was possible to order samples of uranium for a few dollars from Army Surplus catalogues. My father and uncle purchased a specimen, which my grandfather disposed of by burying it in his rose garden, where it presumably seeped into the water table. I spent a good portion of my childhood seeking it out, without success, although I did find other items of interest.

Mirrors

Sitting on a cherry wood stool in their attic room,
the one they converted for the sake of cool air,
the possibility of sunlight and the sound of the river
rising above the thick fields of orange grove

and Australian pines. Ruth is cutting her hair
out of habit. She could afford a beautician now,
Dan has made it at last, but she is used to this
and it gives her triumph, a hard satisfaction.

The face she sees, the face she can't stand,
except when he touches it, has the same contours
and features of the nineteen-year-old bride,
blurred slightly at the corners. Same wide, clear
forehead, same wide, clear eyes. A nose carved
aquiline, made for nobility. The same hair,
or its approximation, worn since nineteen-forty-nine.

The face of someone striving for a return
to stasis. Composed. You would never believe
that passionate lips had ever sucked that white neck.

Dark lips, dark-stubbled,
breathing in hard, stoking up an appetite
that she would never speak of, moving
implacably, ecstatically downward
to hover at her chiffon covered waist.

He'll be coming in soon
from his reclamation work, his job fixing the broken,
making useful the useless, societies' dregs.
Work her man is suited for, being reclaimed himself,
reclaimed by her.
She powders her neck.

The no-longer children are out now:
Danny in medical school, two years early,
John up at Stanford. Their soft youngest
girl, their treasure, out on a date.
All three do well with the children
they're sparking, though only Danny
is dating a name her family would know.
John might still reveal a surprise.
There is always hope.
There is little left for her to do,
but wait.

Her perfume comes
in a small, carved bottle,
blue glass and the scent
of fresh Spring roses.

It feels like a change of seasons,
A warm, slow glow
in this room, though
it is well into Autumn. The seasons
are different here. Their outlines more vague.
There are oranges fruiting
in the yard, beside the new blossoms.
It is Spring, for Ruth, Spring coming late.

Downstairs there is a doorslam,
the high whine of joyous dogs,
feigning misery for love of a pat.
She is decorous now, before her tall glass,
casting her features into calm resolution.
He cannot know that she was waiting.
Forgetting, she dusts her neck, sending
scented talcum out in clouds. The sculptural nobility
of her white flesh.

The bedroom door swings open,
admitting a warm blast, the scent
of good leather. She sees him then,
a slant-smiling reflection, dark eyes,
less hair than he once had, but a trim
hard waist and a look of rejoicing.

There is time now, and the space
to take a long, unstifled breath.
Her swan arms, their blue room,
the watered silk spread on the Queen-sized bed.
His eyes, his dark stubble, his lips
on her neck.

The Kingdom

I The Church Yard

My father was interning as a junior pastor,
stationed in the central Georgia Retardation Center –

it was the mid-seventies, before the birth
of euphemism, when a hard word
divided the oats from the tares and the borders
on the map were more than blurred lines

– a low brick building with narrow
windows, surrounded by waste
trees and untried playgrounds.

He was younger than I am now,
a minister in embryo, dedicated to establishing
the love of God among desolate ruins.
He did not know what humanity was.

Compassion comes naturally to no-one,
that gift springs up in the cooled ashes of fear;
it spreads it roots in those blanched remains.

He followed the white coat through a forest of linoleum
corridors, a rats' nest of mazes, overlaying smells of old sweat,
fresh urine, strong clear pine. Crayons, old food, close noises,
a flurry of motion around his guide's sepulchral calm.

'This is where we keep the children.'
A light cough, an open door, those eyes, all staring,
'The playroom. Made for entertaining.'

Stunted bodies, drool, a few heads
        as soft and conical as remedial
dunce caps. Two little girls with Hurler's syndrome,
their faces warping to caricatures of gargoyle deformity
sat on a square of red carpet walking their dolls.

A teenager in diapers sat slumped in his chair
blowing spit bubbles, laughing at the miracle
of rainbows through his half-focused eyes.

What could he tell them, this boy-priest
who would become my father?
They knew all they ever would
of the subject of God.

But God is not a subject, and He never
has been. Grace is more than academic, it leaves
the intellect in rubble, difficult to learn.

My father stood in that bright room
and felt how awful goodness was.
In this place of broken lives
he could never be the teacher.

He was taught.

II   The Baptist and the Changeling

If Hell is a state of perpetual stasis
then the minister had found it's denizen.
My untried father walked among the bodies
of salvaged children, fed, powdered, diapered, otherwise
forgotten, engaging the few with meaningful words
in stilted conversation. 'Mister see my car?'
His Baptist's fingers rotate a saliva gummed wheel,
'Yes. It is lovely. Drive carefully now.' The exchange
of vague smiles.

He met them all, one by one, waiting for the revelation.
They seemed happy enough, if a little sedated.
All save for a small brown blur of energy,
a small, perfect form running round these tattered
husks, this wasted adolescence.
Despite his training, his warmed through compassion,
he could not help the thought,
What is that real child doing in here? A rose
seemed blooming amidst the scattered waste lands.

The image of health in Dockers and a toddler's jacket,
it drew John on, further in to the playroom
past the worn narthex, the magnetic pull
of the crown of an infant's soft head, seen
from the back. My future father followed, Dantesque,
pursuing those eyes through the dark of the forest.

When the child reached the distant wall, altar-
lit by yellow window-light, he spread out his arms,
a rebounding swimmer, and used the sill to launch
his limber nursling body, racing back, blur-fast and dark
to catch my joyful, untried father proleptically
about the knees. My father cupped that fine, soft head
as lovingly as he would cup my own a decade later.

And, as I would, the small face
turned to meet him,
smiling up.

This is hell.
A man of forty years
who does not know that years have passed.
A face like an infant's, but with crow's-feet,
unearned by any expended emotion.
A body that runs as fast a quicksilver,
and shall continue its fleeting course without
a destination or ending, for another twenty years or so,
before its sudden abysmal failure. A future
of futile pain, uncomprehending screaming,
never changing. For now he still smiles.

We must become as children to enter that good kingdom,
become, but not remain.
There were years in those eyes, but no sense of meaning.
My father twitched once, but made stay his hand,
in the gesture of blessing, acting father-like,
ministerial, to this changeling
which in a better world would be old enough
to father him. This is the way to foster compassion.

It is much to John's credit that when I swam up world ward,
when I set my toddler's feet to, running, meet him,
when I threw my new child's arms around his high knees
he did not recoil. He cradled my head,
hiding his fear,
He looked down and smiled.

III The Altar

This is a story my grandfather tells me.
He worked many years
in vocational rehabilitation, which was I imagine,
something like fishing. Fishing for men,
or their fragments, casting out a strong line, a net,
into the depths of mental illness, drawing something
up to breach the crest and bathe in the light,
or flounder in air, drowning. This story
is not about the drowned.

He worked among broken minds,
broken bodies, learning his own medicinal grace.
One morning he found a man in his net,
ready to clean, or release, ready for judgement.

He said, to me, 'The man was an idiot.
Dribbling. Completely degenerate. I left him fiddling
his fat fingers on my desk. I asked my supervisor,
why bring him to me? He understands nothing.
What can I do for him? He's too dumb to be trained.
I couldn't even teach him how to lay down upholstery.'

When he gets to this part, my grandfather
leans across the table top, grinning at me
black gummed, over his black, twine-bound Bible,
which smells of his sweat, in-ground from decades
of long morning readings. He tells me more in Kentuckian basso,
'Well, my boss finally talked me back into the office.
I gave in and went. Know what I found?'

I know well by now, he knows I know. I tell him, 'No.'
Smiling.

He laughs at me, Nana laughs with him, scrambling
the grits in the never-cleaned pan;
You never soap iron. It takes on the flavour
of the years of your cooking, passes it on
through butter and meat. A meal in endless
re-iteration. We never get tired
of this morning telling.

'The idiot was drooling. It spilled down
all over his chin. He sucked it back up, liquid,
Hur, hur, hur! Like that. Snorting pig-like,
a sow that turned up something real
good.'

My grandfather takes a sip of paint-stripping coffee.
'But damn it, Bethany,
he'd taken apart my radio and laid the parts out,
all across my desk. He was careful, but was I mad?
Was I ever.'

'It took a minute, but I remembered my business enough
to hold it all in. I sat down in my chair
and started talking to him. The fella ignored me.
I might not have been there. But I was.
And I am telling you now the thing that I witnessed.

The idiot put my radio back together in under
five minutes. He fixed it better than it ever was.
Or ever had been.

Eventually I got the story.
His mother didn't want him, and she dropped him off
on the doorsteps of the Retardation Center.
The doctors brought him in and since he was there
and so young, no one ever bothered testing.

People depend a lot on instinct in this sort of thing.
Even doctors. More than they admit.

He grew up in that wasteland, and since he was smart
he took to acting like the people around him.
He learned their behaviours, but he couldn't stop thinking.
He was good at it. Thinking.
The white coats only figured him out
when a night nurse caught him
fixing the television. Said it played better once
he'd been at it than it ever had.
So they brought him to me.'

We break for grace, a ritual that is the best kind
of familiar. Nana serves herself last, takes
less than any of us. Is the last to sit down
the first to rise up. A real Southern lady.
We taste a bit, salty pork,
baked apples, I fiddle the grits round the plates,
untasted.

'He never did use words. I got him a job
as an electrician. Couldn't ever get him to talk.
But you'd better believe he sung with his hands.'

A sigh over a plate this time, the Bible closed
on the sideboard. 'Never forget, girl,
in your life,
the things that you can learn from an idiot.
Don't call another man defective
till you've tried to reach him
from every side.'

This is how we start our morning,
in laughter, in light.
This is the story my grandfather tells me.
Now I'm telling you.
Some things get better with the telling,
like the flavour in an unsoaped pan.

* * *

Ruth

The iron blade is brown , pockmarked,
blunt at the tip. The shaft is slightly curved
like a sickle or unripe plantain, though the edge
has been honed sharp enough to bite through bone.

My father's cousin sharpened it in his grinder,
added a new hand-carved handle of reddish oak,
but the blade is still the one her mother held
a century ago; for Ruth it is almost like touching

her mother's strong fingers, every time she
lifts the blade up. I watch my grandmother
dismember a chicken. The blunt point enters
breastbone, cracking through cartilage

with a broken-nose sound and the kitchen air is filled
with the smell of something wetly female, fleshy,
suddenly exposed. She removes the packet of organs
the butcher replaced, exclaiming over the fact of two hearts

and no kidneys. She will use them for gravy.
Ruth leaves the carcass spread-eagled, riven,
on the naked board and slices the twinned hearts
into identical strips. The iron pan is ancient also,

and has never been touched with scrubber or soap.
A centuries worth of larded meals have permeated
the black, suffusing it with flavours
        going back to Pennsylvania and further,
to Germany where a distant matron welcomed it,

a wedding gift suited for dissuading the fairies.
Ruth heats it a minute on the new easy-clean stove
before adding the dyed butter, telling me, 'You know
when I was a girl the butter was mostly white.

The colour depends on the food the cow gets,
the quality, if they get alfalfa or regular hay.
Sometimes you'd get a pat that tasted of onions,
very strong, garlicky. Good for pasta but not much else.

This why it was so important to keep the cows
out of your garden, not to mention the damage
they could do to your flowers. I think they started
dying it to make it more appealing,

for consumers. So people would think they were getting
something a little nicer than lard.'
The butter has clarified, her white hands
add muscle that hits with a rageful sound,

a billowing steam cloud and the wonderful scent
of boiling fat. She stirs the flesh with a spoon,
the handle gnawed, splintered by my own new teeth,
decades ago. She adds pepper, salt, a pinch of flour.

A splash of milk and there it is, gravy. She pours it
into a china boat, rinses out the greasy pan.
Powdering the sectioned breasts with flour,
heating the oil. 'The secret is to cook it thoroughly

but fast. You have to get the heat right.
Too much and it will spit at you,
you'll end up burnt like I was when the boiler exploded.
The flesh of my arm hung down in strips,

tattered like fabric. It didn't even hurt
at first. There was too much damage. The doctor cut
the skin away with scissors, like he was cutting drapes.
But I was lucky; it healed well under the poultice.'

The chicken turns golden
under the heat, then darkens
to meet the colour of her knife.
I sit in the linoleum-covered chair,

the yellow shade of butter,
worn smooth by our bodies,
mine, and my father's, the cushion thinned
by the bones of generations.

Lear on the Moor

How often does our surface
provide a true mirror for
the weather in our depths? Ole'Doc does not
know that he is asking this as he wedges
his linseed-scented violin beneath his chin folds
and frets at the fingerboard.

He draws the tune
his ear demands, plucking the wires to sweet
reverberations, forced larger by the lashes
of the white horse-hair bow he had custom made
from a dear-departed racing stallion that served
him well in the Derby for three seasons,
but let him down in the end.

He enjoys touches like this, that final thread
of sure control, though he would never
phrase it quite like that. Out loud.
He turns the ancient pages
of music, yellowed and black, crisp at the edges,
loving the hard notes, so definite,
made – in his playing –
completely exact.

It does not matter, to him,
what the author intended.
He only knows he plays it well.
He does not know, as he tightens
the pegs another notch, that the wood
is aching. He does not know why he is thinking of Ruth.

The music swells around him, filling the room
with its single strong voice, his voice.
It covers the sounds of the hired girls in the kitchen,

it covers the sound of his great weight shifting on boards.
He is wearing a red fisherman's sweater,
knitted in cashmere. He does not know that Ruth
will take it from the cloakroom after he is dead,
and warm herself with it for thirty years,
imagining his touch, his distinctive scent
of leather and alcohol.

He sees the music
as thick blue smoke,
from burning coals,
clouding over the uncut pages
of unread books, an ancient medical bag,
deeds, mineral rights, and orders
for mine equipment
on which the ink is still wet.

He will leave the mines to his children:
some of them.
He has read Darwin, determined
the success of the ones that are worthy,
and he has emerged through the decades
of unionisation with hardly a scratch.

He has built up a kingdom
and it does not matter
how well or ill age crowns him. Happiness
is a dream reserved for the undeserving,
the unambitious, who flaunt the orders
of his hands. He knows that joy is compensation.
And yet.

A foul note, startling,
a kink in the thread.
He screws at the neck,
agony in wood, in ivory, in his fingertips

sweetens the tone. He lowers the bow,
contemplating the ängstlich
of the notes, adding in a little acceso,
ma non troppo, spread out,
as fluid as molten sand cooling to glass
across the browning page.

The Ole'Doc wonders
how the weather is in Florida. He has heard
that it is always bright and Spring-like there,
that new life flows, a benign radiation,
where Ruth is. His dissenting, fleeing daughter.
He wonders if this myth is true.

A change might do him some good. His sons
could take over, or the ill-named Loving boy
his good daughter Mary at last agreed
to do her part and wed.
It could be time, now. The King to depart,
leave the kingdom in good hands. The workers
are placid, ready it seems, for a change of command.

It might be time to admit his lost daughter,
into the safe harbour of his fine skilled arms,
to forgive her mistakes, her gross disobedience.
He plucks the string, to test the tune. Ignoring
the harsh twang of its breakage, ignoring
the sting of the backlash as its fury
lashes red marks his cheek.
He is getting older now. His wife, always
a good and loyal partner, has had another stroke,
and she could use a good nurse.

Selkie: The River's Daughter

When I was a child, the hair cut
straight across my forehead,
we lived by a river that fed mangroves,
where the herons speared black snakes
and infant alligators, and the city municipalities,
in the cheapest of wisdom, allowed sewer water
to flood into streams feeding the sheepshead
which grew giant and toxic, scales as big
as the nails on your hand.

I was a creature of that river, plunging down
in my cheap dresses, peeling them off
when the water soaked them too heavy to stand.
I swam through the currents, a knife in my teeth,
bone-handled, it came from great-grandfather,
brought home from the wars. I slaughtered
nothing on those swims, save for
the dragons which rose in my mind. I never took
a lover there on the stream bank, on bed
of palmetto leaves or saw blade, but I found
many real romances on the estuary called
Jacob's Island. Where the drunks slept off
their amethyst wine and the wharf rats formed kings,
tied into knots by their fractured tails,
hung from slick branches.

See what I saw. Look though those eyes,
filth-blinded slits, the colour of sewage,
observe the moment I first loved light.
The sunshine gold in early morning, pouring
through those knife-shaped leaves, the glory
of Zeus poured out on Danaë, made pregnant
by light. That numinous glow, which rose
from the water, made lovely for once, the colour

of silver, new-forged, left to cool on the brace.
I was planted there, drunk on heron wing,
enchanted by fish scale, something took root.
This is the flower.

The roots, which grow from watching,
taste of soil fed by rich water, laden with spoil,
and though it was waste, I was not wasted.
Coming home again, here, my feet in the spoilage,
the only locality, unmapped, where all that is beautiful
can possibly grow. What looks foul feels fair
in this light. And those bones you despise
feed the soil where the flowers of the true reality
take root and grow.

Thickets

We are gathered in the forest,
camped between the stands
of blackberry, in a clearing
of the pines. I am twelve
years old and wild. In one week
my father shall send me
to an orphanage in South Carolina.
For now, there are the woods.

None of the extended family knows.
To them, I am a strange one, but gifted
with my words. Always talking,
to myself, the dogs, or to the trees, no one
is quite sure. We spend our time
in extended hikes, in mountain climbing,
in panning the riverbeds for gems
and fool's gold. I spend my time
sticking close to Nana, who tolerates
my bird's nest hair, my prepubescent
unwashed smell.

She tells me stories from the mountains;
poor widows with ten children
and no shoes, who dyed their hair with
the tannin from pummelled roots
and covered their bare feet with flour sacks
to make ready for the long walk to church.

She tells of her father, the country doctor,
who amputated a miner's crushed leg
in situ, severing bone-shards and tendons
pinned under the beam, without ether or candle
in the moist pitch darkness of the mine.
She tells how that man lived and later fathered
thirteen children on a teenager he married
who was born eyebrowless and blind.

She talks to me by fireside,
as she makes the three large meals;
cooking slabs of beef skewered on spits
for cousins, and fat-burst sausages
roasted on straightened coat-hangers
to eat crusted by the stale rolls bought
at the camp store, which also sells fireworks
illegally, regardless of season.
I hang on her speech, hiding,
for a brief while, from my future
in her past.

She falls to silence,
needing a rest, she waves me off
and I flee fast to bracken,
fleeing as the doe does
down narrow deer-paths,
through thicket and briar,
to the place no man might follow.

And there are creatures,
black-nosed and hoofed,
who curl their brown flanks
in the green thickets, lying
down in sweet timothy grass
to lick to life the soft-ribbed heaving
of a newborn's spotted flank.

They know my scent, unclean
and proto-female, they know the rhythms
of my movements.
They do not stir or startle when I burst
into their circle. They are calm,
and I calm with them. Listening quietly,
for they have their stories, too,
albeit different from Nana's narrative.

I sleep there,
waking after dark to a supper
of plump blue huckleberries
and a long walk back down
a narrow silver thread, beaten brazen
by hoof-fall. I arrive back at camp the moment
the moon does. Avoiding my father,
Nana takes me to hand and in a move
reminiscent of baptism, leads
her soiled progeny to the water-filled
trough, to the frigid pump.

The water is drawn from the heart of the earth,
the planet's own blood, so cold it feels
as though I am burning. Her fingers
gather in my tangles, unwinding
the thread, measuring it out, as though
gauging my life. She does not soften
my character with soap, just the tang
of new water, and through that torrent,
looking up, I see the moon. Full, full
and open, casting it's golden nimbus,
pure and forest-held, around us both.

The End of the Ride

Riding fast to a funeral, wheels speeding,
wheels in wheels, my Nana's dressed for travelling:
skirt, gloves, hat, that worn leather purse
clutched blue in her lap. We are sitting in the rear seat
of the Cadillac, listening to road and implacable wheel-hum,

sixteen hours to go before our arrival
at the site of the death, the place of burial.
Voyaging is hard on my grandmother,
and not just because the deceased
is her second-eldest brother but all long rides

are difficult for her who is happiest circumscribed,
muffled by house. The cause of this journey must never
be mentioned. Linger on the cheerful, the homely,
the bright. Talk about eating; where to do it,
what to get. Settle on the dollar chilli at Wendy's,

hot with crackers, served in a yellow cup.
Don't think. Tell funny stories.
Apologise again to me for my Spring break ruined
by flying to Florida just in time to drive up north.
Do not listen to my absolving words, respond to the tone,

leaning in to my arm. Flirt like a cat being stroked.
Agonize over the nuance of your words,
with more fervour than you would otherwise express,
if you were less afraid. Take my bare hand in your soft,
cool fingers. Squeeze harder than you meant.

Do not think about death.

Tell funny stories.
The time your son, my father, whom you call John-Nelson,
frightened the housekeeper by mounting something he found
in a cave on the handle of the hall closet vacuum cleaner,
Plugging it in so that it would rush out at her

when she opened the door.
There it was, some Indian's skull.
Talk about old peg-leg Johnson
with his tarpaper house on the side
of the mountain, who never went down

into the mine, and had a succession
of women to play-act as wives. Tell how he lived
on a government pension, drinking steadily
and never bathing. Wonder out loud how he got
all those women. Answer yourself

with a reminder of their limited choices.
Some of them were lucky to get even that.
Remind me of the awful penalty for falling,
for any mistake. When you say it, squeeze my hand.
Call him a reprobate, redeemed only by his

aid at funerals. For forty years in town,
he dug all the graves. Wonder who did it for him
when his time came. Wonder what happened
to the parade of his women. Wonder what the cleaners
made of the government issue prosthetics he kept

stacked behind the stove like cord wood
and never used, favouring the splintered peg. Tell how it
and the long daisy chain of wounded women
never allowed him, or anyone, to be soothed,
or forget.

Do not talk about your brothers, or your vanished
mountain life. Do not think about your dying sister,
bloated and baffled with one leg lost to diabetes.
Look at me with wide blue cats-eyes beneath
your maintained forties fringe, kept auburn,

neatly curled. Do not speak about your aging.
Repeatedly forget my name and lineage
and call your husband my father.
You will never know how much I, in understanding,
love that. Or how much I wish that it were so,

that you were both mother and grandmother,
that I could enlarge our time together,
on this earth.
But Nana, I do ponder what is coming, I hold
it like treasure, in my mind and heart.

You squeeze my hand between your gloves
and come back to that subject, in spite of yourself,
time after time, after time, as the wheels feast on road.

Cordelia

You had a favourite chair,
scuffed, overstuffed leather
that came from your father;
the fragment he chose,
Lear-like, to leave to
the one who loved him best,
the one he cast out.

It is the brown chair you nursed him in
the year he was dying,
the one he almost never stirred from
after his last stroke.
You fed him, bathed him, kept
him warm and entertained
at the cost of your own family.

He took it as a tribute,
something you owed,
and he paid you back contempt
spiced with the occasional hard word.
The same stone he always gave you
when you held your hand
out for good bread.

You were the only child of his
who bothered to come.
When he called,
you came running,
out of more than
the usual cradle-trained duty,
although the year you spent
lodged in his house
nearly wrecked your marriage.

You came, because
you really loved.

        * * *

You eat lunch in the living room
from a polished tray with the inset
table-mat, watching
CSI on television, engrossed
in spite of yourself
in this safe brutality;
actors, scripted, with fake blood.
You flog your brain
to figure out
these riddles.
Such is your outlet.

You still eat there, lunch times,
though you bought
a new chair
when your father's wore out,
black springs torn
through scuffed leather.

It has dark blue
upholstery and reclines,
the padding dense
and well-stuffed,
too big for your body.

It is a comforting size
and now you watch *Bones*
every day but Sunday,
at twelve o'clock
in a chair that feels

nearly the same,
clothed in a new skin,
retaining its ghosts.

* * *

The two of you are still in love,
sixty years since your meeting
on that ivied porch.
It is a minor miracle.

I caught you once,
on the wooden kitchen counter,
the one you have replaced
with easy-clean black marble
that makes the room look dark
in spite of the wallpaper,
in the pattern of china,
blue and white.

You were swept up,
lip-locked
like hormonal
teenagers.
Crocuses in winter,
this late Spring of your life.

Once you told me
you could not resist his lips.
But you had drunk some wine then,
and that might have loosened
your hold on your tongue.

* * *

I am hurtling
towards thirty and will probably
always eat with my fingers.

It is not your fault
that I am the wrong class.

I remind you,
on the cellular level,
on the level of blood,
of the choice you made
when you chose who you wed.

He came from good family,
a line of good farmers,
minor businessmen,
soldiers, sharp shooters,
but there is a difference
between good family
and the men who own the mines,
a difference of bloodline,
of shade.

* * *

The family who birthed you,
your living siblings,
continue their punishment
for forgetting,
for mistaking your father
for the mask that he wore,
for being guileless enough,
or innocent, shamming,
or all three together,
to mistake him for a country doctor
and not the owner of the mines.

After all, he did go visit people.
He did have a cart, a horse and a battered
leather bag. He did see patients in his office
at the rear of the house.
You sterilized his instruments
on the stove hob, and held the limbs he stitched.

How many babies
did you help him deliver?
How many crushed miners' legs
did he amputate while you held the ether?
How many lives did he save?
And does it really matter much
that he took the wounded men's mineral rights
if they lacked the cash to pay?

It was nothing more than business,
how everybody gets ahead,
how a country doctor becomes mine owner,
and yet remains a doctor, pledged
to health and not to Mammon.
The American way. And your father
was determined to be American,
but not of *this* race

            * * *

This was the story
that you needed
to marry your man;

your father,
the jovial family doctor,
who loved you,

and had an *interest* in mining,
without much caring
for the black bottom-line.

You needed this
to blur the lines,
to forge a link
between your lives.

You needed your daddy
to care for people
more than coal seams,
and so he did, and does,
for you.

Your gift is not spinning,
but in editing the thread,
snipping the ends and tying together
the loose fibres
that other hands have spun.

    * * *

And so you got the life
of your own choosing,
forgetting the early years
of punishment,

when Dan, your dark beloved,
was on the do-not-hire lists
in the town your father owned,
and you sweated away your youth
in one of the mine stores
for wages less than believable
to the miners who saw you
driven to this same shop

a year ago
by a servant in black livery.
They laughed at you,
behind their hands; you furnished
your floorless house
in cast-offs and fire-damaged scraps.
And then you had the babies.

    * * *

Such details slip out
when you forget to pay attention,
like all unlanced stores of pus
suppurating at last;
but I am, in part, for remembering,
for doctoring,
for making wounds whole.
I never forget.

And sometimes
there must be an edge to loving.
You must focus enough
on misery to let the poison out.
This is a fragment of what I am,
a sterilised scalpel,
this cut.

Rembrandt, A Portrait

There is a portrait by the man in Kansas City,
a minor rendering of an aristocrat, a dashing of genius,
exuding the light he is known for, caught in the brown curls
of a noble young man who bears the face of my father.

That was surprising. Seeing John, my father, there
in baroque garb, splashed out in oils,
his face, nonetheless, and my father beside it,
smiling like a lottery winner, in awe of discovery.

The same brow-ridged forehead, same
brown crescent eyes that can't help rejoicing.
The nose both splayed wide and fleshy
above sensuous lips that fit me well, being a poet,
but lend the look of something earthly,
obscenely vulnerable to the face of a man
dedicated to the service of God.

There is little chance that we are related
to this Dutchman, if he is Dutch. Our blood
has been mingled from other sources:
German mostly with Native American and a fragment
of English and, for me at least, a dousing of Scottish,
courtesy of the blood of my mother.

John bought a print of this painting in the gift shop
of the Nelson Atkins Museum, titled: Unknown.
He hung it up in the guest room of their new house
in Louisiana, a place called Monroe. We call it

his Unauthorized Portrait. It is mounted beside
a real painting, done decades ago, in Rembrandt's style,
new venturesome light, cast in amateur oils
which he commissioned from an artist in Virginia
at the start of his ministry, when he was younger
than I am now.

It has travelled across four seas; from North America,
to Scotland, the Philippines, and back again
by way of California and China,
travelling on bootstrings, voyaging in spite
of his straining threadbare wallet. Other belongings

lost, broken or stolen, furniture smashed
so that only this portrait remains, carried across
the time stream. By now enough waters have flowed
out of his grasp that there isn't any wonder
at the fact that neither portrait really looks
much like him at this late date. But when I stand

between them on my infrequent visits,
people who don't expect much wonderment in life
lean hard on chairs, and suck in their breath
at the hard shock of recognition, gasping
at the works of the Masters, Old and New,
which I have joined in creative amalgamation,
recording and recorded, noble and artist, both ends together,
who cast their images on the seas of the world.

Caught in the Teeth

'It happened like this, Bethany, I came down
this morning to open the Book,' Popie wags
his bald pate at the Bible on the cabinet, not noticing
the mistake of names, though Nana bristles by the sink,
'and I felt something in there with my tongue tip,
    kind of catching,
like a piece of popcorn kernel, which they tell me
I can't have anymore. But never mind.'

He takes another sip of paint-stripping coffee,
being careful with his lips against the rim,
mouthing the china like a horse would, after
getting hold of a fresh, sweet carrot. Nana
hovers between us and the stove, fiddling
with nothing, there is nothing to cook.

She has always been frightened of mortality,
or evidence of it. She sees this as proof
that even her best china, her silver plate,
will pass away. The fact that we will is beyond her.
She jumps just this way when she catches
her mind reeling that way.

'Anyway, I set to digging at it with my tongue,
it felt real strange, half disconnect, half pressure,
and the next thing I knew, they'd all spurted out.
All of them. The whole top row.' He smiles now,
and it is ghastly; the heart of rotten fruit,
flyblown road kill, an aged, toothless mouth.
'Like I was spitting seeds.'

Nana sucks in air, to draw time back, in recall or fact.
'Did it hurt, Popie?' I look at the dark oak table top,
at blue plastic placemats, at the glass dish
red-streaked, glistening, left from the baked apples,
anyplace not his mouth. He reaches out with worm-veined
warm hands, to touch me. His voice a rumble, with a lisp.
'No, no. I didn't feel anything. Just wonderment.'

'The feeling you get when you're out hunting
and you see something; an eagle, hawk or a snow-
white fox, something too good to shoot,
running through winter-light, so clear and so blinding,
that you feel lucky enough to have lived to see.
It should have been awful, but it wasn't.' He smiles again,
but not for effect. Covering time's most recent wound
with fingers and thumb.

'Anyway, I cannot get your Nana to look
at me, so it's a good thing the dentist called me back.
They can see me Monday morning. While you're
at the gym. I asked if I should bring the teeth,
thought maybe they could mount them in resin,
glue them back in. The dentist – she's a lady
weightlifter. Ever hear such a thing?
But she's pretty enough for all that – said that I should
just chuck them out before they spoil. I can't quite do that yet,
can't go around divesting myself of myself
without thought. So I've set them in a dish
in our bathroom. By the sink. They're kind of pretty,
after you get used to them. Your Nana doesn't like it.'

I am not quite sure how to answer; I take a sip
from my cup. Nana is standing in the light
of the window. Florida Spring-light, golden and green
through new leaves, clothing her in radiance
that clings to her skin. She smiles to see it,
thin hair glimmering, she smiles at her man.
'There are different kinds of pretty', she tells him,
laying her lips on his cheek. She cannot, yet, bring herself
to kiss that changed, that well-loved mouth.
She needs time to adjust.

Acknowledgements

I would like, first and foremost, to thank my grandparents Dan and Ruth Pope. They are the true authors of these stories, if not the poems that contain them. I owe them more than my existence.

This same holds true for my parents, John Nelson and Joy Marie Pope, who raised me up, aided by my foster mother Librada (Virgie) Castro.

I would like to thank my husband, Matthew Clarke, whose enduring love and support made the writing possible and whose judicious criticism helped to make it good.

I would like to thank the poet Tiffany Atkinson, who taught me so much and I would also like to thank Menna Elfyn and Matthew Francis for their continued love, guidance and support.

My thanks also go to Agnes Cserhati who saw my potential, and of course, importantly, Maria McCarthy and Bob Carling of Cultured Llama who saw something in my writing that was worthy of publication and who helped to make the best shine out.

Cultured Llama Publishing

hungry for poetry
thirsty for fiction

Cultured Llama was born in a converted stable. This creature of humble birth drank greedily from the creative source of the poets, writers, artists and musicians that visited, and soon the llama fulfilled the destiny of its given name.

Cultured Llama is a publishing house, a multi-arts events promoter and a fundraiser for charity. It aspires to quality from the first creative thought through to the finished product.

Cultured Llama's first venture in 2011 was the publication of *strange fruits*, a poetry collection by Maria C. McCarthy, in association with WordAid.org.uk. All profits from the sale of *strange fruits* go to Macmillan Cancer Support.

The Cultured Llama logo and the cover image of *strange fruits* were designed by Maggie Drury. Maggie writes novels and plays, paints – mostly semi-abstract oils and acrylics – and makes woodcuts.

www.culturedllama.co.uk

Also published by Cultured Llama

strange fruits
by Maria C. McCarthy

Paperback; 72pp; 129 x 198 mm;
978-0-9568921-0-2; July 2011;
Cultured Llama (in association with
WordAid.org.uk)

Maria is a poet of remarkable skill, whose work
offers surprising glimpses into our 21st-century
lives – the 'strange fruits' of our civilisation or
lack of it. Shot through with meditations on the past and her heritage
as 'an Irish girl, an English woman', *strange fruits* includes poems
reflecting on her urban life in a Medway town and as a rural resident
in Swale.

Maria writes, and occasionally teaches creative writing, in a shed at
the end of her garden.

All profits from the sale of *strange fruits* go to Macmillan Cancer Sup-
port, Registered Charity Number 261017.

'Maria McCarthy writes of the poetry process: "There is a quick-
ening early in the day" ('Raising Poems'). A quickening is cer-
tainly apparent in these humane poems, which are both natural
and skilful, and combine the earthiness and mysteriousness of
life. I read *strange fruits* with pleasure, surprise and a sense of
recognition.'

Moniza Alvi, author of *Europa*

Lightning Source UK Ltd.
Milton Keynes UK
UKOW052240300512

193653UK00001B/1/P